TAYLOR SWIFT

LEGENDS ALPHABET

Words by Robin Feiner

Aa

A is for **A**ll Too Well (10 Minute Version). In 2012, Tay Tay sang tearfully of all the wild ups and downs with her boyfriend. They danced under the autumn leaves and in the refrigerator light, but it wasn't meant to last. Eleven years later, All Too Well: The Short Film won the Best Music Video award at the Grammys.

Bb

B is for **B**lank Space.
In this 8x platinum hit from her amazing 1989 album, T-Swift's ready for her next relationship. Over an electropop rhythm that gets feet tapping and heads bopping, she tells a future boyfriend, 'I've got a blank space, baby... and I'll write your name!'

C is for Cardigan.
Taylor thanked her Swifties in 2020 by giving them two surprise albums. This slow burn from Folklore, the first of those albums, is all about the beauty and tears of teen romance. With Cardigan's instant success, Tay proved— once again—to be the most legendary songwriter of her generation.

Dd

D is for Look What You Made Me **D**o. 'I'm sorry, but the old Taylor can't come to the phone right now!' In this proudly sassy song, Swift showed the world she can be a bad girl. From lying in a bath of diamonds to wearing a full-body fishnet outfit, she confronts the haters who shunned her away, announcing her epic return.

E is for Enchanted. Tender and wistful, strumming her acoustic guitar, Tay sings of the emotions we feel after meeting someone truly enchanting. She's wonder-struck, blushing all the way home, hoping, 'Please don't be in love with someone else!' But how could they possibly choose anyone other than her?

Ff

F is for Fearless.
As an 18-year-old, the ever-strong Taylor recorded this tale of the perfect first date. As the first track on her classic Fearless album, this song shows how beautiful it can be to allow yourself to fall in love and how, when you have a new crush, the streets look a little different just after it's rained.

Gg

G is for Getaway Car. 'Should've known I'd be the first to leave!' On this hit, Tay sings of saying goodbye to a toxic ex and starting something new. But this relationship was doomed from the beginning as she comes to learn that 'nothing good starts in a getaway car.'

Hh

H is for Anti-Hero.
'I wake up screaming from dreaming, one day I'll watch as you're leaving.' This single from Tay's Midnights album shows her at her weakest. She's as relatable as she ever gets—scared, sad, and searching for meaning in her life... It's no surprise Anti-Hero became one of 2022's best-selling singles!

**I is for Shake It Off.
Our pop-country princess has dealt with non-stop rumors and lies ever since bursting onto the scene. This crazy-catchy, billboard-topping banger from her 1989 album was all about being bigger than all that negativity. Whether it's the fakers, haters, players, or heartbreakers, Tay promises to just Shake It Off.**

J is for The Joker and The Queen. Slowly and in harmony, T-Swift and her good friend Ed Sheeran sing about how nothing can keep true lovers apart—not even a Queen and a Joker. He showed her his true self, and she fell head over heels. 'I showed you my hand, and you still let me win. And who was I to say that this was meant to be?'

K is for I **K**new You Were Trouble. Taylor's been through her fair share of charmers and heartbreakers, so she knows trouble when she sees it. Sometimes, that trouble is too much to resist. But after this chart-topping, legendary, 7x platinum track, it's clear to everyone that Taylor got the last laugh.

L is for Lover.
A forever type of love with someone who will accept us, scars and all—isn't that what we're all looking for? On this 2019 track from her album of the same name, Tay had finally found love. 'Can I go where you go? Can we always be this close, forever and ever?' Sadly not, but we get the idea.

M is for **M**ine.
With this warm and upbeat
ballad, Taylor proclaims
her love for being in love to
anyone who will hear her.
In a mega-hit music video
drenched in sunlight and
good vibes, T-Swizzle is all
smiles, romance, and affection
with the man of her dreams.
'You are the best thing that's
ever been mine!'

N is for We Are **N**ever Ever Getting Back Together. 'You go talk to your friends, talk to my friends, talk to me!' It's Miss Americana at her most empowering, telling the world, once and for all, that her former flame is on his own, and that she is better off without him. Her decision to be happily single produced this legendary hit—her first-ever #1 on the Billboard Hot 100.

O is for **O**ur Song. Taylor was just a newcomer back in 2007. But with this track, she broke into the country scene, becoming the youngest person ever to write and record a song that made it to #1 on the Hot Country Songs chart. Who knew she'd be singing it to thousands of screaming fans 16 years later? Taylor did.

P is for **P**aper Rings.
On this upbeat tune, Tay sings about how a big, shiny ring isn't what shows a girl she's loved—it's the person behind the ring! As everyone's favorite pop queen once said, 'This song talks about true love, and if you really find true love, you probably don't really care what the symbolism of that love is.' Truer words have never been spoken.

Q is for Question...?

'Did you leave her house in the middle of the night? Did you wish you'd put up more of a fight?' When a relationship ends, it's easy to ask questions like these. But in this slow and thoughtful song, Taylor shows that what a heartbroken lover wants more than anything is answers.

R is for Ready for It? Back in 2017, Tay Tay returned to the pop scene with Reputation, another legendary new album. She also had a new bad-girl persona, and this bold, powerful, confident hit. Many changes were happening around her— but Taylor showed she was ready for anything.

S is for Love Story. Recorded in 2008 and re-recorded in 2021, Love Story is one of the greatest songs Tay has ever written. It's about forbidden love, craving that one special person, and wanting to run away with the man of your dreams. 'You'll be the prince, and I'll be the princess, it's a love story, baby, just say yes.' We say yes, Taylor!

T is for You Need to Calm Down. Internet trolls? Ew! Taylor knows better than anyone how annoying haters can be. But she's not bothered—she's done up in her bikini and fluffy jacket, chilling by the pool, telling everyone to calm down! Aside from being super-catchy, this popular track is also an LGBTQIA+ anthem!

U is for Me! feat. Brendon Urie. Taylor's a cat mom, a fashion icon, and the youngest female artist to ever win Album of the Year at the Grammys. She also knows all about self-worth, and with help from Panic! at the Disco's incredible Brendon Urie, she dove head-first into this classic tune about the importance of being and loving yourself.

V is for The **V**ery First Night. With cheerful lyrics and a catchy acoustic melody, Taylor sings about how beautiful things once were. She's reminiscing over that first date and first night together, when sparks turned to romance, and when a crush blossomed into love: 'Not trying to fall in love, but we did, like children running.'

W is for Willow.
This metaphorical love song was the hit single on evermore, the second of Taylor's surprise albums in 2020. Tay sings of life being like a willow tree, its thin branches swaying in the wind, its roots spreading beneath the soil. That's how special she feels when she finds a love meant to last.

X is for exile.
This legendary duet dives deeper into Tay Tay's heart than anything before it. She's a girl saying goodbye with a tearful, gentle voice, and Bon Iver's a boy with a soulful baritone asking, 'What went wrong?' With such heart-tugging lyrics, it's no surprise critics call exile one of her greatest tunes to date.

Y is for **Y**ou Belong with Me. In this playful and catchy song, Taylor wonders how her love interest could want a girl who's not right for him. With over 1.4 billion YouTube streams, it's a legendary anthem for girls around the world wondering the same thing. 'She wears short skirts, I wear T-shirts, she's cheer captain, and I'm on the bleachers!'

Z is for I Don't Wanna Live Forever ft. **Z**ayn. Over a high-pitched melody and electro-R&B rhythm, Taylor and Zayn sing of that classic love/hate relationship with the lover you just can't give up. Even though they know they're better off apart, they can't stop longing for each other: 'I just wanna keep calling your name... till you come back home!'

The ever-expanding legendary library

EXPLORE THESE LEGENDARY ALPHABETS & MORE AT WWW.ALPHABETLEGENDS.COM

TAYLOR SWIFT LEGENDS ALPHABET
www.alphabetlegends.com

Published by Alphabet Legends Pty Ltd in 2023
Created by Beck Feiner
Copyright © Alphabet Legends Pty Ltd 2023

Printed and bound in China.

9780645851489

ALPHABET LEGENDS